G000278774

CHRISTMAS BLESSINGS

Also by Helen Steiner Rice

Just For You

Heart Gifts

Lovingly

Prayerfully

Thankfully

Somebody Loves You

Loving Promises

And the Greatest of These is Love

Remembering With Love

A Time to Love

Loving Thoughts

Christmas Blessings

FROM

HELEN STEINER RICE

❄ ❄ ❄

Hutchinson

Copyright © 1991 by Virginia J. Ruehlmann and The Helen Steiner Rice Foundation

The right of Helen Steiner Rice to be identified as the author of this work
has been asserted by her in accordance with the Copyright
Designs and Patents Act. 1988

All rights reserved

5 7 9 10 8 6 4

This book is sold subject to the conditon that it shall not, by way of trade or otherwise, be lent,
resold, hired out, or otherwise circulated without the publisher's prior consent in any form of binding
or cover other than that in which it is published and without a similar condition including this
condition being imposed on the subsequent purchaser

This edition first published in the United Kingdom in 2000 by Hutchinson

The Random House Group Limited
20 Vauxhall Bridge Road, London SW1V 2SA

Random House Australia (Pty) Limited
20 Alfred Street, Milson Point, Sydney,
New South Wales 2061, Australia

Random House New Zealand Limited
18 Poland Road, Glenfield
Auckland 10, New Zealand

Random House (Pty) Limited
Endulini, 5a Jubilee Road, Parktown 2193, South Africa

The Random House Group Limited Reg. No. 954009
www.randomhouse.co.uk

A CIP catalogue record for this book is avilable
from the British Library

Papers used by Random House
are natural, recyclable products made from wood grown in
sustainable forests. The manufacturing processes conform to
the environmental regulations of the country of origin

ISBN 0 09 179417 X

The Scripture quotations in this book are taken from the Revised Standard Version of the Bible,
Copyrighted © 1946, 1952, 1971, by the Division of Christian Education of the National Council of
the Churches of Christ in the United States of America, and are used by permission. All rights
reserved.

Typeset by Deltatype, Birkenhead, Wirral
Printed and bound by Nørhaven Book A/S, Denmark

Dedicated to

fans, friends, family,
former co-workers, and neighbors
of Helen Steiner Rice
and
especially and gratefully
to her sister,
Gertrude Steiner,

in memory of the many Christmases shared

The Helen Steiner Rice Foundation

God knows no strangers, He loves us all
The poor, the rich, the great, the small.
He is a Friend who is always there
To share our troubles and lessen our care.
No one is a stranger in God's sight,
For God is love and in His light
May we, too, try in our small way
To make new friends from day to day.

Whatever the celebration, whatever the day, whatever the event, whatever the occasion, Helen Steiner Rice possessed the ability to express the appropriate feeling for that particular moment in time.

A happening became happier, a sentiment more sentimental, a memory more memorable because of her deep sensitivity to put into understandable language the emotion being experienced. Her positive attitude, her concern for others, and her love of God are identifiable threads woven into her life, her works . . . and even her death.

Prior to her passing, she established the HELEN STEINER RICE FOUNDATION, a nonprofit corporation whose purpose is to award grants to worthy charitable programs that aid the elderly, the needy, and the poor. In her lifetime, these were the individuals about whom Mrs. Rice was greatly concerned.

Royalties from the sale of this book will add to the financial capabilities of the HELEN STEINER RICE FOUNDATION, thus making possible additional grants to various qualified, worthwhile, and charitable programs. Because of her foresight, her caring, and her deep convictions, Helen Steiner Rice continues to touch a countless number of lives. Thank you for your assistance in helping to keep Helen's dream alive.

Virginia J. Ruehlmann, Administrator
The Helen Steiner Rice Foundation
Suite 2100, Atrium Two
221 E. Fourth Street
Cincinnati, Ohio 45201

CONTENTS

Christmas is . . .

Introduction

Christmas, that most beautiful and highly cherished feast of the Christian year, is celebrated in remembrance of the Nativity of our Lord.

Unfortunately, there are times when the true meaning of Christmas is lost in the hustle-bustle-hurry-scurry days of December.

The role Christmas plays in an individual's life depends on the interpretation of the event and varies from person to person and family to family. There are, however, certain qualities, such as the miracle and spirit of the day, its effect, its glory, and its joy, that are appreciated by all believers. To promote, promulgate, and pass these values on from generation to generation should be the goal of each Christian.

Helen Steiner Rice understood this challenge. She grasped these qualities and beautifully expressed them in her works, in heartwarming sentiments and easy-to-comprehend terms.

May this collection of her verses assist you to capture and to retain the true meaning of Christmas, its values, and the enjoyment that can radiate from it.

Virginia J. Ruehlmann

For many more than I care to remember
I have always looked forward to this time in December
As an annual reunion in heart and in thought
For renewing the friendships a long life has brought.
And this is a love link that keeps me in touch
With the wonderful people who have helped me so much
Whose friendship and kindness I will never forget . . .
For my life has been shaped by the people I've met.
And my books and my verses belong not to me
They reflect the dear folks who have unconsciously
Inspired my thinking in a myriad of ways
And encouraged my efforts with their prayers and their
  praise.

HELEN STEINER RICE

Christmas is the Miracle of Christ's Birth
a Virgin conceiving, miraculous and amazing
a star shining, angels praising
shepherds kneeling, throngs adoring
joy increasing, spirits soaring

VJR

❄   ❄   ❄

Now the birth of Jesus Christ took place in this way. When his mother Mary had been betrothed to Joseph, before they came together she was found to be with child of the Holy Spirit; and her husband Joseph, being a just man and unwilling to put her to shame, resolved to divorce her quietly. But as he considered this, behold, an angel of the Lord appeared to him in a dream, saying, 'Joseph, son of David, do not fear to take Mary your wife, for that which is conceived in her is of the Holy Spirit; she will bear a son, and you shall call his name Jesus, for he will save his people from their sins.' All this took place to fulfil what the Lord had spoken by the prophet:

'Behold, a virgin shall conceive and bear a son,
and his name shall be called Emmanuel'

(which means, God with us). When Joseph woke from sleep, he did as the angel of the Lord commanded him; he took his wife, but knew her not until she had borne a son; and he called his name Jesus.

Matthew 1:18–25

Unto Us a Child Is Born

God sent the little Christ Child
So men might understand
That a little Child shall lead them
To that unknown Promised Land.
For God in His great wisdom
Knew that men would rise to power
And forget His holy precepts
In their great triumphal hour.
He knew that they would question
And doubt the Holy Birth
And turn their time and talents
To the pleasures of this earth.
But every new discovery
Is an open avenue
To more and greater mysteries,
And man's search is never through.
For man can never fathom
The mysteries of the Lord
Or understand His promise
Of a heavenly reward.
For no one but a little Child
With simple faith and love

Can lead man's straying footsteps
To higher realms above!

❈   ❈   ❈

Was It Really So?

A star in the sky, an angel's voice
Telling the world –
Rejoice! Rejoice!
But that was centuries and centuries ago,
And we ask today
Was it really so?
Was the Christ Child born in a manger bed
Without a pillow to rest His head?
Did He walk on earth
        and live and die
And return to God to dwell on high?

We were not there to hear or see,
But our hopes and dreams
     of eternity
Are centered around that holy story
When God sent us
His Son in glory
And life on earth has not been the same,
Regardless of what
     the skeptics claim,
For no event ever left behind
A transformation of this kind.
So question and search and doubt,
     if you will,
But the story of Christmas
     is living still.

The Miracle of Christmas

The wonderment
     in a small child's eyes,
The ageless awe
     in the Christmas skies,
The nameless joy
     that fills the air,
The throngs that kneel
     in praise and prayer . . .
These are the things
     that make us know
That men may come
     and men may go,
But none will
     ever find a way
To banish Christ
     from Christmas Day.
For with each child
     there's born again
A mystery that baffles men.

❆ ❆ ❆

He Was One of Us

He was born as little children are
     and lived as children do,
So remember that the Savior
     was once a Child
     like you,
And remember that He lived on earth
     in the midst of sinful men,
And the problems of the present
     existed even then.
He was ridiculed and laughed at
     in the same
     hearbreaking way
That we who fight for justice
     are ridiculed today.
He was tempted . . . He was hungry . . .
He was lonely . . . He was sad . . .
There's no sorrowful experience
     that the Savior
     has not had;
And in the end He was betrayed
     and even crucified,

For He was truly One of us –
He lived on earth
      and died;
So do not heed the skeptics
      who are often
      heard to say,
'What does God up in heaven
      know of things we face today?'
For, our Father up in heaven
      is very much aware
Of our failures and shortcomings
      and the burdens
      that we bear;
So whenever you are troubled
      put your problems in God's hand
For He has faced all problems
And He will understand.

A Christmas Thought

If there had never been a Christmas
    or the Holy Christ Child's birth,
Or the angels singing in the sky
    of promised peace on earth
What would the world be like today
    with no eternal goal,
What would the temporal body be
    without a living soul?
Just what would give us courage
    to push on when hope is dead
Except the Christmas message
    and the words our Father said –
'In love I send My only Son
    to live and die for you,
And through His resurrection
    you will gain a new life, too.'

❄   ❄   ❄

The Promise of Heaven

I know how you'll feel when the Christmas
      bells ring,
But here is a thought to which you can cling.
This is the birthday of Jesus whose love
Assures you of meeting your loved ones
      above.
And this glorious story of our Savior's birth
Is our promise of heaven after this earth.

The blessings of Christmas are many,
More then words can express,
Enough to fill every longing heart
With untold happiness.
And the greatest of all blessings
Is the Christmas revelation
That Jesus Christ was born this day
To bring the world salvation.
And that is why this message
Is written here to say
That you are wished the blessings
Of the Holy Christmas Day.

What Would We Face This Christmas Morn If Jesus Christ Had Not Been Born?

In this world of violence
    and hatred and greed
Where men lust for power
    and scorn those in need,
What could we hope for
    and where could we go
To find comfort and courage
    on this earth below
If in Bethlehem's manger
    Christ had not been born
Many centuries ago
    on that first Christmas morn.
For life everlasting
    and eternal glory
Were promised to man
    in the Christmas story!

❄ ❄ ❄

Christmas

A Baby was born in a manger
      while a bright star shone down from above.
And the world learned the depths of God's mercy
      and the comfort and strength of His love.
May the thought of that long-ago Christmas
      and the meaning it's sure to impart,
Bring a wonderful message of comfort
      and a deep new peace to your heart.

God, Make Us Aware

God, make us aware
    that in Thy name
The Holy Christ Child
    humbly came
To live on earth
    and leave behind
New faith and hope
    for all mankind.
And make us aware
    that the Christmas story
Is everyone's promise
    of eternal glory.

❋   ❋   ❋

Christmas is the Peace of Faith
bells ringing, folks churchgoing
　　　choirs singing, warm wishes flowing
　　　joy to the world and silent nighting
　　　peace on earth — calm and quieting

　　　　　　　　　　　　　　VJR

Therefore the Lord himself will give you a sign.
Behold, a young woman shall conceive and bear a son,
and shall call his name Immanuel . . .

> For to us a child is born,
>   to us a son is given;
> and the government will be upon his shoulder,
>   and his name will be called
> 'Wonderful Counselor, Mighty God,
>   Everlasting Father, Prince of Peace.'

Isaiah 7:14; 9:6

> But you, O Bethlehem Ephrathah,
>   who are little to be among the clans of Judah,
> from you shall come forth for me
>   one who is to be ruler in Israel,
> whose origin is from of old,
>   from ancient days.

Micah 5:2

What Is Christmas?

Is it just a day
>   at the end of the year?
A holiday filled
>   with merry good cheer?
A season for presents —
>   both taking and giving?
A time to indulge
>   in the pleasures of living?
Are we lost in a meaningless,
>   much-muddled daze
That covers our minds
>   like a gray autumn haze?
Have we closed our hearts
>   to God and His love?
And turned our eyes
>   from the bright star above?

O Father in heaven, renew and restore
The real, true meaning
  of Christmas once more,
So we can feel in our hearts again
That 'Peace on earth, goodwill to men'
Is still a promise
  that man can claim
If he but seeks it in Thy name.

❈ ❈ ❈

Faith

Unless you become as children
And love Me as they do,
You cannot enter My kingdom,
For the door is closed to you.
For faith is the key
  to heaven
And only God's children hold
The key that opens the gateway
To that beautiful City of Gold.
For only a child yet unblemished
By the doctrines and theories of man
Is content to trust
  and love Jesus
Without understanding His plan.

The Miracle of Christmas

Miracles are marvels
      that defy all explanation
And Christmas is a miracle,
      and not just a celebration.
For when the true significance
      of this so-called Christmas story
      penetrates the minds of men
And transforms them with its glory,
Then only can rebellious man
      so hate-torn with dissension
      behold his adversaries
With a broader new dimension —
And that is why God sent His Son
      as a Christmas gift of love
So that wickedness and hatred
      which the world had so much of,
Could find another outlet
      by following in Christ's way
And discovering a new power
      that violence can't outweigh.

❋ ❋ ❋

God So Loved the World
That He Gave His Only Begotten Son
as a Christmas Gift to Everyone

Our Father up in heaven,
  Long, long years ago,
Looked down in His great mercy
  Upon the earth below
And saw that folks were lonely
  And lost in deep despair
And so He said, 'I'll send My Son
  To walk among them there,
So they can hear Him speaking
  And feel His nearness, too,
And see the many miracles
  That faith alone can do.
For if man really sees Him
  And can touch His healing hand
I know it will be easier
  To believe and understand.'

So whenever we have troubles
  And we're overcome with cares
We can take it all to Jesus,

For He understands our prayers.
For He, too, lived and suffered
    In a world much like our own,
And no man can know the sorrow
    That Jesus Christ has known.
And whatever we endure on earth
    Is so very, very small
When compared to God's Beloved Son
    Who was sent to save us all.
And the blessed reassurance
    That He lived much as we do
Is a source of strength and comfort
    And it gives us courage, too.
And that is why on Christmas.
    God sent His only Son
To teach mankind the wonder
    Of the words, 'Thy will be done.'
And through the countless ages
    The Holy Christ Child's birth
Is our promise of salvation
    And our hope of peace on earth!

May the blessings of this season,
   So old, yet ever new,
Bring you again the knowledge
   That God abides with you.

❄   ❄   ❄

A Child's Faith

'Jesus loves me, this I know
For the Bible tells me so' –
Little children ask no more,
   For love is all
   they're looking for,
And in a small child's shining eyes
The faith of all the ages lies –
And tiny hands and tousled heads
   That kneel in prayer
   by little beds
Are closer to the dear Lord's heart
And of His kingdom more a part

Than we who search, and never find,
        The answers to
        our questioning mind –
For faith in things we cannot see
Requires a child's simplicity
For, lost in life's complexities,
        We drift upon
        uncharted seas
And slowly faith disintegrates
While wealth and power accumulate –
For the more man learns, the less he knows,
And the more involved his thinking grows
And, in his arrogance and pride
        No longer is
        man satisfied
To place his confidence and love
With childlike faith in God above –
O Father, grant once more to men
        A simple childlike
        faith again
And, with a small child's trusting eyes.
May all men come to realize
That faith alone can save man's soul
        And lead him to
        a higher goal.

Christmas

C is for the Christ Child
      a Child of love and light

H is for the Heavens that were
      bright that holy night

R is for the Radiance
      of the star that led the way

I is for the lowly Inn
      where the Infant Jesus lay

S is for the Sheperds
      who beheld the Christmas star

T is for the Tidings
      the angels told afar

M is for the Magi
      with their gifts of myrrh and gold

$\mathcal{A}$ is for the Angels
       who were awesome to behold

$\mathcal{S}$ is for the Savior
       who was born to save all men

And together this spells CHRISTMAS
       which we celebrate again.

In Christ All Men May Live Again

Let us all remember
When our faith is running low,
Christ is more than just a figure
Wrapped in an ethereal glow —
For He came the dwelt among us
And He knows our every need,
He loves and understands us
And forgives each sinful deed —
He was crucified and buried
And rose again in glory
And His promise of salvation
Makes the wondrous Christmas story
An abiding reassurance
That the little Christ Child's birth
Was the beautiful beginning
Of God's plan for peace on earth.

❊　❊　❊

We've Come a Long Way
Since that First Christmas Night

We've come a long way
  since that first Christmas night
When led by a star
  so wondrously bright
The Wise men journeyed
  to find the place
That cradled the Christ Child's
  beautiful face –
But like lost sheep
  we have wandered away
From God and His Son
  who was born Christmas Day,
And instead of depending
  on God's guiding hand
Ingenious man has assumed
  full command

Like the Prodigal Son
     who seeks to be free
From the Heavenly Father
     and His holy decree –
But life without God
     is corroding man's soul,
Weakening his spirit,
     and distorting his goal,
And unless we return
     to our Father again
We will never have peace
     and goodwill among men –
And the freedom man sought
     will make him a slave
For only through God
     is man strong, free, and brave.
So let us return
     to our Father and pray
That Christ is reborn
     in our hearts Christmas Day.

❄ ❄ ❄

Live Christmas Every Day

Christmas is more than the end of the year
More than a time for presents and cheer
More than a time for happy meetings
More than a time for exchanging greetings
More than the tinsel that hangs on the tree
More than the baubles and glitter we see
More than a time for mere happiness
More than small words can ever express

Christmas is one day we find it is good
To live the way that we always should
A day when man tries to be generous and kind
A day when he sees with his heart, not his mind

And that is the way we should live all the year
Not ony a few days when Christmas is here
For that is the way God wants us to live
Sharing the joy that comes when we give

For then and then only will restlessness cease
And all of the world will be finally at peace
For the tidings of Christmas can only come true
When Christmas is lived every day the year through.

God Grant Us Hope
and Faith and Love

Hope for a world
    grown cynically cold,
Hungry for power
    and greedy for gold.

Faith to believe
    when within and without
There's a nameless fear
    in a world of doubt.

Love that is bigger
    than race or creed,
To cover the world
    and fulfill each need.

God, grant these gifts
    to all troubled hearts
As the old year ends
    and a new year starts.

❆ ❆ ❆

Glory to God in the Highest

'Glory to God in the highest
And peace on earth to men' –
May the Christmas song
      the angels sang
Stir in our hearts again
And bring a new awareness
That the fate of every nation
Is sealed securely in the hand
Of the Maker of Creation . . .
For man,
      with all his knowledge,
His inventions, and his skill,
Can never go an inch beyond
The Holy Father's will.
For, greater
      than the scope of man
And far beyond all seeing,
In Him who made
      the universe,
Man lives and has his being.

❄   ❄   ❄

A Christmas Prayer for Peace

We pray to Thee, our Father,
     as Christmas comes again,
For peace among all nations
     and goodwill among all men.
Give us strength and courage
     to search ourselves inside
And recognize our vanity,
     our selfishness, and pride.
For the struggle of all ages
     is centered deep within
Where each man has a private war
     that his own soul must win.
For a world of peace and plenty
     of which all men have dreamed,
Can only be attained and kept
     when the spirit is redeemed.

❄ ❄ ❄

Christmas is the Warmth of Friendships
letter writing, card sending
   news exciting, goodwill extending
   neighbors gathering, friendly greetings
   manger scenes, community meettings
          VJR

. . . the angel Gabriel was sent from God to a city of Galilee named Nazareth, to a virgin betrothed to a man whose name was Joseph, of the house of David; and the virgin's name was Mary. And he came to her and said, 'Hail, O favored one, the Lord is with you!' But she was greatly troubled at the saying, and considered in her mind what sort of greeting this might be. And the angel said to her, 'Do not be afraid, Mary, for you have found favor with God. And behold, you will conceive in your womb and bear a son, and you shall call his name Jesus.

He will be great, and will be called
        the Son of the Most High;
and the Lord God will give to him
        the throne of his father David,
and he will reign over the house of Jacob for ever;
and of his kingdom there will be no end.'

And Mary said to the angel, 'How shall this be, since I have no husband?'

> And the angel said to her,
> 'The Holy Spirit will come upon you,
> and the power of the Most High will
>   overshadow you;
> therefore, the child to be born will be called holy,
> the Son of God.

Luke 1:26–35

A Christmas Message —
the Magic of Love

Love is like magic
And it always will be,
For love still remains
Life's sweet mystery.

Love works in ways
That are wondrous and strange
And there's nothing in life
That love cannot change.

Love can transform
The most commonplace
Into beauty and splendor
And sweetness and grace.

Love is unselfish,
Understanding, and kind,
For it sees with its heart
And not with its mind.

Love is the answer
That everyone seeks
Love is the language
That every heart speaks
Love is the message
That was sent to the earth
On that first Holy Christmas
That heralded Christ's birth!

❋   ❋   ❋

Gift of Friendship

When you ask
        God for a gift,
be thankful if He sends
        Not diamonds,
        pearls, and riches –
        but the love of
        real true friends.

❋   ❋   ❋

Christmastime Is Friendship Time

At Christmastime our hearts reach out
To friends we think of dearly
And checking through our friendship lists,
As all of us do yearly,
We stop awhile to reminisce
And to pleasantly review
Happy little happenings
And things we used to do,
And though we've been too busy
To keep in touch all year,
We send a Christmas greeting
At this season of good cheer.
So Christmas is a lovely link
Between old years and new
That keeps the bond of friendship
Forever unbroken and true.

❄ ❄ ❄

Where Can We Find Him?

Where can we find the Holy One?
Where can we see His only Son?
The Wise Men asked,
     and we're asking still,
'Where can we find this Man
     of goodwill?'
Is He far away in some distant place,
Ruling unseen
     from His throne of grace?
Is there nothing on earth that man can see
To give him proof of eternity?

It's true we have never looked on His face,
But His likeness shines forth
        from every place,
From the hand of God is everwhere
Along life's busy thoroughfare.
And His presence
        can be felt and seen
Right in the midst of our daily routine,
The things we touch and see
        and feel
Are what make God so very real.

❋　❋　❋

Helen Steiner Rice enjoyed keeping in touch with her many fans and friends. Each Christmastime she composed and sent special greetings to those in her list. Reminisce as you read the sentiments she expressed in those messages throughout the years.

✳   ✳   ✳

May Christmas this year, amid chaos,
cruelty, and conflict, be a blessed
instrument through which we can find
comfort and courage and cheer in the
communion of our hearts.

May we discover this Christmas, the
sustaining powers of a strong faith,
and the abiding values of courage,
heroism, honor, fellowship, and freedom.

May our material gifts be less
and our spiritual gifts greater.

'Peace on earth, goodwill to men' is
not an empty dream, it is the miracle
of Christmas – and such miracles are
made of faith and brave hearts.

May God bless America and you, and
may the New Year find us all not only
safe but free.

Helen Steiner Rice
December 25, 1942

In a world grown weary with
war, Christmas shines out
like a candle of courage and
comfort amid the darkness of
destruction.

Nineteen hundred and forty-four
years ago, the world heard the words,
'Peace on earth, goodwill
toward men,' and as we
await another Christmas, it is
with a gleam of hope that God
will grant the fulfillment of this
message that has been ringing
down through the years.

May this Christmas be a beacon
light to a better world, and may
the New Year bring us peace, founded
in freedom, and grant us the strength
born of suffering to build a world
that war can never touch again.

Helen Steiner Rice
Christmas, 1944

I have a list of folks I know, all written in a book . . .
And every year when Christmas comes, I go and take a look . . .
And that is when I realize that these names are a part . . .
Not of the book they're written in, but of my very heart . . .
For each name stands for someone who has crossed my path
    sometime . . .
And in that meeting they've become the rhythm in each rhyme . . .
And while it sounds fantastic for me to make this claim . . .
I really feel that I'm composed of each remembered name . . .
And while you may not be aware of any special link . . .
Just meeting you has shaped my life a lot more than you think . . .
For once I've met somebody, the years cannot erase . . .
The memory of a pleasant word or of a friendly face . . .
So never think my Christmas cards are just a mere routine . . .
Of names upon a Christmas list, forgotten in between . . .

For when I send a Christmas card that is addressed to you . . .
It's because you're on that list of folks whom I'm indebted to . . .
For I am but the total of the many folks I've met . . .
And you happen to be one of those I prefer not to forget . . .
For if I've known you many years or only just a few . . .
In some way, be it large or small, I owe myself to you . . .
And every year when Christmas comes, I realize anew . . .
The best gift life can offer is meeting folks like you . . .
So Merry, Merry Christmas and no words can suffice . . .
To say how much your friendship means to

Helen Steiner Rice.
Christmas, 1949

Again it's Christmas and the year's at an end,
And once again it is time to send
Greetings and gifts and words of cheer
To those who we know and those we hold dear . . .
And so I come as in years before
To knock again on your heart's door,
And I say, 'Heart's door,' as no figure of speech
But because it's your heart that I want to reach . . .
For, unless the door of your heart swings wide
This message I send you at Christmastide
Is nothing more than an artist's design,
Bringing a few rhyming words of mine . . .
But these words I write you are meant to be
Much more than a casual greeting from me,
They come each year as a symbol of
The great Christmas gift that was given for love
Which all too often is hidden from view
In the glamorized, advertised hullabaloo —
So my wish for you is not gifts of gold
That you can unwrap for the world to behold
But I'm hoping your home and heart are bright,
Not with glittering gifts, but an inner light,

For the lights of Christmas are not on a tree,
They're deep in the hearts of you and me . . .
And I want you to know that it's folks like you
Who light lights in my heart and other hearts, too
And my heart reaches out to yours today
With a wish too big for small words to say,
A wish that the meaning of Christmas will stay
And light candles of love that will not fade away
But will glow in your heart and home all year
And light all of the lives that you come near —
For the light of the world can only be lit
By the lights in the hearts that are part of it.

Helen Steiner Rice
Christmas, 1952

It's Christmas and time
        to greet you once more,
But what can I say
        that I've not said before
Except to repeat
        at this meaningful season
That I have a deeply
        significant reason
For sending this greeting
        to tell you today
How thankful I am
        that you passed my way.
For I happen to have
        a deep feeling love
For even the people
        I know little of.
The stranger who smiles
        as we pass on the street
Or the business acquaintance
        I happen to meet
Are more than just people
        with a name and a face,

They are part of God's love
              and each one has a place
In the plan of our Father
              which is much greater than
All of the plans
              and inventions of man.
And so may the knowledge
              that God's everywhere,
And as close to you always
              as one little prayer,
Help you to know
              that you're never alone,
For God is your Father
              and you're one of His own.
And may Christmas bring you
              a lovely heart lift
And may Christ Himself
              be your Christmas gift.

Helen Steiner Rice
Christmas, 1956

The years bring many changes in many ways, it's true . . . . and perhaps I should change and modernize, too . . . . Perhaps I should stop sending long Christmas rhymes . . . . And change to a greeting more in tune with the times . . . . Something that's casual and impersonally terse . . . . Instead of a warm little heart-to-heart verse . . . . For I have been told that in this modern day . . . . A heart-to-heart greeting is strictly passé . . . . But I can't help feeling there's already too much . . . . Of that heartlessly cold and impersonal touch . . . . In business and all walks of living today . . . . And nothing remains to brighten our way . . . . For what is there left to make the heart sing . . . . When life is a cold and mechanical thing . . . . And what have we won if in reaching this goal . . . . We gain the whole world and lose our own soul . . . . And so, though I'm open to much ridicule . . . . As one who belongs to an outmoded school . . . . I still am convinced that kindness, not force . . . . Is the wiser and better and more Christlike course . . . . For no modern world of controlled automation . . . . No matter how perfect its regimentation . . . . Can ever bring joy or peace to the earth . . . . Or fulfill the promise of Jesus Christ's birth . . . . For progress, and money, and buttons to press . . . . And comfort and leisure and toil that is less . . . . Cannot by themselves make a world that is free . . . . Where all live together in true harmony . . . . For it isn't the progress made by man's mind . . . . But a sensitive heart that is generous and kind .... That can lighten life's burden and soften life's sorrow .... And open the way to a better tomorrow .... And a better tomorrow is my wish and my prayer .... Not only for you but for folks everywhere .... And I hope that this Christmas will bring you and yours .... The joy that's eternal and the peace that endures .... But with life's many changes one fact remains true .... I'm richer for having known someone like you.

Helen Steiner Rice
Christmas, 1957

Our Father, up in heaven,

            hear this Christmas prayer:

May the people of all nations

            be united in Thy care,

For earth's peace and man's salvation

            can come only by Thy grace

And not through bombs and missiles

            and our quest for outer space.

For until all men recognize

            that the battle is the Lord's

And peace on earth cannot be won

            with strategy and swords,

We will go on vainly fighting,

            as we have in ages past,

Finding only empty victories

            and a peace that cannot last.

But we've grown so rich and mighty

            and so arrogantly strong,

We no longer ask in humbleness –

            'God, show us where we're wrong.'

We have come to trust completely

            in the power of man-made things,

Unmindful of God's mighty power
          and that He is King of kings.
We have turned our eyes away from Him
          to go our selfish way,
And money, power, and pleasure
          are the gods we serve today.
And the good green earth God gave us
          to peacefully enjoy,
Through greed and fear and hatred
          we are seeking to destroy.
O Father, up in heaven,
          stir and wake our sleeping souls,
Renew our faith and lift us up
          and give us higher goals,
And grant us heavenly guidance
          as Christmas comes again —
For, more than guided missiles,
          all the world needs guided men.

Helen Steiner Rice
Christmas, 1961

This is more than a card at the end of the year . . . Coming to wish you the season's good cheer . . . It's a message of thanks I find hard to convey . . . For there's so little space and so much to say . . . For so many people in so many ways . . . Have put new encouragement into my days . . . I just can't help thinking, and frequently, too . . . How grateful I am to know people like you . . . And this truly has been a most wonderful year . . . With wonderful tributes from folks far and near . . . Letters of praise, so kindly expressed . . . I just can't help feeling both humble and blest . . . For only God, working through people like you . . . Could answer my prayers and make all this true . . . For the people I meet and work with and see . . . Inspire the things which are written by me . . . And the beauty folks find in a word, phrase, or line . . . Is their soul's reflection just mirrored in mine . . . And there's no time like Christmas with its meaningfulness . . . To recall and remember and attempt to express . . . How much it has meant through the year 'Sixty-two' . . . To have known and been helped by people like you . . . And I hope God will bless you as we start 'Sixty-three' . . . And return all the kindness you've shown people like me.

Helen Steiner Rice
Christmas, 1962

Nothing would make me happier
　　　　or please me any better
Than to write you my thanks
　　　　in a long, friendly letter —
For being remembered
　　　　at the holiday season
By someone like you
　　　　gave my heart ample reason
To count all my blessings,
　　　　and your friendship is one,
For without fans and friends
　　　　the writing I've done
Would lose all its meaning,
　　　　its warmth, and sincereness,
For how could I write
　　　　without feeling a nearness
To all the dear people
　　　　who interpret each line
With their own love and kindness
　　　　which becomes part of mine —

So more than you know
   I thank God up above
For fans, friends, and family
    and their gifts of love.

      Helen Steiner Rice
      January, 1967

My Christmas gift
            is a gift of love —
For all of my poems
            are woven of
Words that I borrow
            from our Father above
He gives them to me
            and I give them to you
And through Him we meet
            and communicate, too,
And as Christmas comes
            and another year ends
I thank God once more
            for my fans and my friends
And may my future writings
            be most worthy of
Your fanship and friendship
            as we share in His love.

                    Helen Steiner Rice
                    Christmas, 1968

I am planning to walk
                    on a path yet untrod,
Content that my future
                    will be determined by God —
But it doesn't take Christmas
                    to make me remember,
Nor are my good wishes
                    confined to December —
But as day follows day
                    and thought follows thought,
I'll think of the joy
                    that your friendship has brought,
And may the books I have written
                    and the words I have spoken
Be a spiritual bond . . .
                    unchanged and unbroken.

Helen Steiner Rice
Christmas, 1970

My Christmas Prayer

Shed Thy light upon us
>> as Christmas comes again
So we may strive for peace on earth
>> and goodwill among men
And, God, in Thy great wisdom,
>> Thy mercy, and Thy love,
Endow man with the virtue
>> that we have so little of . . .
For unless we have humility
>> in ourselves and in our nation,
We are vain and selfish puppets
>> in a world of automation,
And with no God to follow
>> but the false ones we create,
We became the heartless victims
>> of a Godless nation's fate . . .
Oh, give us ears to hear Thee
>> and give us eyes to see,
So we may once more seek Thee
>> in true humility.

May the knowledge that Someone cares
and hears our prayers sustain you in
these dark hours of uncertainty. And may
God's love and His joy flow around the
troubled world and may you and I together
help to make this a reality. This is the
Christmas wish and prayer of

Helen Steiner Rice

Dear Fans, Friends, and Loved Ones

I just want to make it clear
        that constantly throughout the year
I catch a glimpse of God's great grace
        or see the likeness of His face
In something that is said or done
        that makes my day a better one
Because a smile or deed or word
        or something that I saw or heard
Transformed a dull and dreary minute
        by putting heavenly sunshine in it.
And so my Christmas prayer once more
        is coming to your friendly door
To hope that God, in love, will bless
        your heart and home with happiness
And may He hear the prayer I pray
        and bless you specially,
        Christmas Day!

Helen Steiner Rice

THE GLOW OF GIVING

Christmas is the Glow of Giving
shoppers shopping, children gift making
mothers cooking, grandmothers baking
fathers tree trimming, families caring
homeless remembered, heartfelt sharing

VJR

And in that region there were shepherds out in the field, keeping watch over their flock by night. And an angel of the Lord appeared to them, and the glory of the Lord shone around them, and they were filled with fear.

And the angel said to them, 'Be not afraid; for behold, I bring you good news of a great joy which will come to all the people; for to you is born this day in the city of David a Savior, who is Christ the Lord. And this will be a sign for you: you will find a babe wrapped in swaddling cloths and lying in a manger.' And suddenly there was with the angel a multitude of the heavenly host praising God and saying,

'Glory to God in the highest,
and on earth peace among men with whom he is pleased!'

Luke 2:8–14

Giving

Christmas is a season of giving
And giving is the key to living.
So let us give ourselves away,
Not just at Christmas but every day
And remember a kind and thoughtful deed
Or a hand outstretched in time of need
Is the rarest of gifts, for it is a part
Not of the purse, but a loving heart.
And he who gives of himself will find
True joy of heart and peace of mind.

May the Gifts of Christmas Be Yours

The richest gifts
Are God's to give,
May you possess them
As long as you live,
May you walk with Him
And dwell in His love
As He sends you good gifts
From heaven above.

God's Love Is the True
Gift of Christmas

There are many gifts of Christmas
That are purchased with silver and gold,
Dazzling in their splendor
And breathtaking to behold
But the one true gift of Christmas
Is a gift from God above
Assuring every mortal man
Of God's enduring love.
For with this Christmas gift of love
Our spirit is redeemed,
And man at last possesses
The peace of which he dreamed.

❄   ❄   ❄

Give Lavishly!
Live Abundantly!

The more you give, the more you get
The more you laugh,
    the less you fret
The more you do unselfishly,
The more you live abundantly.

The more of everything you share,
The more you'll always
    have to spare
The more you love, the more you'll find
That life is good
    and friends are kind.

For only what we give away,
Enriches us from day to day.
So let's live Christmas through the year
And fill the world
    with love and cheer.

❄ ❄ ❄

The Christmas Tree

Listen ... Be quiet ... Perhaps you can hear
the Christmas tree speaking ... soft and clear:

I am God's messenger of love
And in my Christmas dress
I come to light your heart and home
With joy and happiness —
I bring you pretty packages
And longed-for gifts of love,
But most of all I bring you
A message from above —
The message Christmas angels sang
On that first Christmas night
When Jesus Christ the Father's Son
Became this dark world's light —
For though I'm tinsel-laden
And beautiful to see
Remember, I am much, much more
Than just a glittering tree,
More than a decoration
To enhance the Christmas scene,
I am a living symbol

That God's love is evergreen —
And when Christmas Day is over
And the holidays are through
May the joyous spirit of Christmas
Abide all year with you —
So have a Merry Christmas
In the Blessed Savior's name
And thank Him for the priceless gifts
That are ours because He came.

❄ ❄ ❄

The Mystery and the Miracle of His Creative Hand

In the beauty of a snowflake,
Falling softly on the land,
Is the mystery and the miracle
Of God's great, creative hand.
For what better answers are there
To prove His Holy Being
Than the wonders all around us
That are ours just for the seeing!

A Christmas Prayer

Our Father who art in heaven
Hear this Christmas prayer,
And if it be Thy gracious will
May joy be everywhere.
The joy that comes from knowing
That the Holy Christ Child came
To bless the earth at Christmas
For Thy sake and in Thy name.
And with this prayer there comes a wish
That these holy, happy days
Will bless you and your loved ones
In many joyous ways.

The Priceless Gift
of Christmas

Christmas is a heavenly gift
    that only God can give,
It's ours just for the asking
    for as long as we shall live.
This priceless gift of Christmas
    is meant just for the heart,
And we receive it only
    when we become a part
Of the kingdom and the glory
    which is ours to freely take,
For God sent the Holy Christ Child
    at Christmas for our sake
So man might come to know Him
    and feel His presence near
And see the many miracles
    performed while He was here.
This priceless gift of Christmas
    is within the reach of all —
The rich, the poor, the young and old,
    the greatest and the small.
So take His priceless gift of love,

reach out and you receive,
And the only payment that God asks
is just that you believe.

❉　❉　❉

Practice Kindness

Kindness is a virtue
given by the Lord,
It pays dividends in happiness
and joy is its reward,
For, if you practice kindness
in all you say and do,
The Lord will wrap His kindness
around your heart and you.
And wrapped within His kindness
you are sheltered and secure,
And under His direction
your way is safe and sure.

Christmas Is a Season for Giving

Christmas is a season
For gifts of every kind,
All the glittering, pretty things
That Christmas shoppers find,
Baubles, beads, and bangles
Of silver and of gold –
Anything and everything
That can be bought or sold
Is given at this season
To place beneath the tree
For Christmas is a special time
For giving lavishly,
But there's one rare and priceless gift
That can't be sold or bought,
It's something poor or rich can give
For it's a loving thought –
And loving thoughts are something
For which no one can pay
And only loving hearts can give
This priceless gift away.

✽ ✽ ✽

What Christmas Means to Me

Christmas to me is a gift from above –
    a gift of salvation born of God's love.
For far beyond what my mind comprehends
    my eternal future completely depends
On that first Christmas night centuries ago
    when God sent His Son to the earth below,
For if the Christ Child had not been born
    there would be no rejoicing on Easter
    morn.
For only because Christ was born and died,
    and hung on a cross to be crucified,
Can worldly sinners like you and me,
    be fit to live in eternity.
So Christmas is more than getting and giving,
    it's the why and the wherefore of infinite
    living,

It's the positive proof for doubting God never,
        for in His kingdom life is forever.
And that is the reason that on Christmas Day,
        I can only kneel down and prayerfully say,
'Thank You, God, for sending Your Son,
        so when my work on earth is done,
I can look at last on Your holy face,
        knowing You save me alone by Your grace.'

Peace
on earth
will come to stay
When we live
Christmas
every day.

❄ ❄ ❄

Christmas Glitter

With our eyes
we see the glitter
of Christmas,
With our ears
we hear the merriment,
With our hands
we touch the
tinsel-tied trinkets,
But only
with our hearts
can we feel
the miracle of it.

The Gift of God's Love

All over the world at this season,
Expectant hands reach to receive
Gifts that are lavishly fashioned,
The finest that man can conceive.
For, purchased and given at Christmas
Are luxuries we long to possess,
Given as favors and tokens
To try in some way to express
That strange, indefinable feeling
Which is part of this glad time of year
When streets are crowded with shoppers
And the air resounds with good cheer.
But back of each tinsel-tied package
Exchanged at this gift-giving season,

Unrecognized often by many,
Lies a deeper, more meaningful reason.
For, born in a manger at Christmas
As a gift from the Father above,
An Infant whose name was called Jesus
Brought mankind the gift of God's love.
And the gifts that we give have no purpose
Unless God is part of the giving,
And unless we make Christmas a pattern
To be followed in everyday living.

Let Us Bring Him
a Gift of Joy
as Did the Little Drummer Boy

As once more we approach
      the birthday of our King —
Do we search our hearts
      for a gift we can bring,
Do we stand by in awe
      like the small drummer boy
Who had no rare jewels,
      not even a toy,
To lay at Christ's crib
      like the Wise Men of old
Who brought precious gifts
      of silver and gold —
But the drummer boy played
      for the Infant Child
And the Baby Jesus
      looked up and smiled,
For the boy had given
      the best that he had
And his gift from the heart
      made the Savior glad —

And today He still smiles
        on all those who bring
Their hearts to lay
        at the feet of the King.

❋   ❋   ❋

The Way to a Better World

We can only live in peace
When we learn to love each other
And accept all human beings
With the compassion of a brother . . .
It takes the Christ of Christmas
To change man's point of view,
For only through the Christ Child
Can all men be born anew . . .
So in the Christmas story
Of the Holy Christ Child's birth
Is the answer to a better world
And goodwill and peace on earth.

Periodically, the Steiner family enjoyed extended visits from Helen's Grandmother Bieri. It was she who encouraged Helen to memorize passages from the Bible, passages of Scriptures never to be forgotten but rather retained and used frequently in her life and in her works.

Grandmother Bieri was often asked by Helen to relate the folktale of Father Martin, written originally by Ruben Salliens and retold by Leo Tolstoy. Years later, as an adult, Helen adapted the story and expressed it in poetic form. She titled it, 'The Story of the Christmas Guest.'

The Christmas Guest

When I was a child I loved to hear
    This story my grandma told each year.
She told it in her native tongue,
    And I was very, very young,
But yet this story seemed to be
    Filled with wonderment for me.
For in my childish heart there grew
    The dream that I might see Him, too,
For He might call on me this way
    So I must watch for Him each day.
And that is why 'the Christmas Guest'
    Is still the story I love best –
And I retell it to you now,
    For I can't help but feel somehow
That children everywhere should hear
    The story Grandma told each year . . .
For Christmas Day in doubly blest
    When Jesus is our Christmas Guest!

❀   ❀   ❀

The Story of the Christmas Guest

It happened one day at the year's white end . . . two neighbors called on an old-time friend . . . and they found his shop so meager and mean . . . made bright with a thousand boughs of green . . . and Conrad was sitting with face a-shine . . . when he suddenly stopped as he stitched a twine . . . and said, 'Old friends, at dawn today . . . when the cock was crowing the night away . . . the Lord appeared in a dream to me . . . and said, "I am coming your Guest to be" . . . so I've been busy with feet astir . . . strewing my shop with branches of fir . . . the table is spread and the kettle is shined . . . and over the rafters the holly twined . . . and now I will wait for my Lord to appear . . . and listen closely so I will hear . . . His step as He nears my humble place . . . and I open the door and look in His face.'

So his friends went home and left Conrad alone . . . for this was the happiest day he had known . . . for, long since, his family had passed away . . . and Conrad had spent a sad Christmas day . . . but he knew with the Lord as his Christmas Guest . . . this Christmas would be the dearest and best . . . and he listened with only joy in his heart . . . and with every sound he would rise with a start . . . and look for the Lord to be standing there . . . in answer to his earnest prayer.

So he ran to the window after hearing a sound . . . but all that he saw on the snow-covered ground . . . was a shabby beggar whose shoes were torn . . . and all of his clothes were ragged and worn . . . So Conrad was touched and went to the door . . . and he said, 'Your feet must be frozen and sore . . . and I have some shoes in my shop for you . . . and a coat that will keep you warmer too' . . . So with grateful heart the man went away . . . but Conrad noticed the time of day . . . he wondered what made the dear Lord so late . . . and how much longer he'd have to wait . . . when he heard a knock and ran to the door . . . but it was only a stranger once more . . . a bent, old woman with a shawl of black . . . a bundle fo twigs piled on her back . . . she asked for only a place to rest . . . but her voice seemed to plead, 'Don't send me away . . . let me rest for a while on Christmas Day' . . . So Conrad brewed her a steaming cup . . . and told her to sit at the table and sup.

But after she left he was filled with dismay . . . for he saw that the hours were passing away . . . and the Lord had not come as He said He would . . . and Conrad felt sure he had misunderstood . . . when out of the stillness he heard a cry . . . 'Please help me and tell me where am I' . . . So again he opened his friendly door . . . and stood disappointed as twice before . . . it was only a child who had wandered away . . . and was lost from her family on Christmas Day . . . Again Conrad's heart was heavy and sad . . . but he knew he would make this little child glad . . . so he called her in and wiped her tears . . . and quieted all her childish fears . . . then he led her back to her home once more . . . but as he entered his own darkened door . . . he knew that the Lord was not coming today . . . for the hours of Christmas had passed away.

So he went to his room and knelt down to pray . . . and he said, 'Dear Lord, why did You delay? . . . What kept You from coming to call on me? . . . For I wanted so much Your face to see' . . . when soft in the silence a voice he heard . . . 'Lift up your head for I kept My word . . . Three times My shadow crossed your floor . . . Three times I came to your lonely door . . . for I was the beggar with bruised, cold feet . . . I was the woman you gave to eat . . . and I was the child on the homeless street.'

Christmas is the Joy of Remembering
children sledding, groups ice-skating
      eyes twinkling, smiles radiating
      hot chocolate simmering, spirits glowing
      popcorn popping, snowflakes snowing
      fires in the hearth, burning and embering
      nostalgic memories, fond remembering

                          VJR

Now when Jesus was born in Bethlehem of Judea in the days of Herod the king, behold, wise men from the East came to Jerusalem, saying, 'Where is he who has been born king of the Jews? For we have seen his star in the East, and have come to worship him.' When Herod the king heard this, he was troubled, and all Jerusalem with him; and assembling all the chief priests and scribes of the people, he inquired of them where the Christ was to be born. They told him, 'In Bethlehem of Judea; for so it is written by the prophet. . . .

When they had heard the king they went their way; and lo, the star which they had seen in the East went before them, till it came to rest over the place where the child was. When they saw the star, they rejoiced exceedingly with great joy; and going into the house they saw the child with Mary his mother, and they fell down and worshiped him. Then, opening their treasures, they offered him gifts, gold and frankincense and myrrh.

Matthew 2:1–5, 9–11

Rejoice! It's Christmas!

May the holy remembrance
     of the first Christmas Day
Be our reassurance
     Christ is not far away.
For on Christmas He came
     to walk here on earth,
So let us find joy
     in the news of His birth.

And let us find comfort
     and strength for each day
In knowing that Christ
     walked this same earthly way.
So He knows all our needs
     and He hears every prayer
And He keeps all His children
     always safe in His care.

And whenever we're troubled
and lost in despair
We have but to seek Him
and ask Him in prayer
To guide and direct us
and help us to bear
Our sickness and sorrow,
our worry and care.
So once more at Christmas
let the whole world rejoice
In the kowledge He answers
every prayer that we voice.

Christmas Is
a Season of Kindness

May the kindly spirit of Christmas
Spread its radiance far and wide
So all the world may feel the glow
Of this Holy Christmastide
And then may every heart and home
Continue through the year
To feel the warmth and wonder
Of this season of good cheer
And may it bring us closer
To God and to each other
'Til every stranger is a friend,
And every man a brother.

Christmas and
the Christ Child

In our Christmas celebrations
Of merriment and mirth
Let's not forget the miracle
    Of the
Holy Christ Child's birth
For in our festivities
It is easy to lose sight
    Of the
Baby in the manger
And that holy silent night.

And we miss the mighty meaning
And we lose the greater glory
        Of the
Holy little Christ Child
And the blessed Christmas story
        If we don't
Keep Christ in Christmas
And make His love a part
Of all the joy and happiness
That fill our home
        and heart.

The Presence of Jesus

Jesus came into this world
> one glorious Christmas Eve.
He came to live right here on earth
> to help us to believe.
For God up in His heaven
> knew His children all would feel
That if Jesus lived among them
> they would know that He was real
And not a far-off stranger
> who dwelt up in the sky
And knew neither joys nor sorrows
> that make us laugh and cry
And so He walked among us
> and taught us how to love
And promised us that someday we
> would dwell with Him above.
And while we cannot see Him
> as they did, face-to-face,
We know that He is everywhere,
> not in some far-off place.

※　※　※

God Bless You at Christmas

God bless you at Christmas
And go with you through the year,
And whenever you are troubled
May you feel His presence near;
May the greatness of His mercy
And the sweetness of His peace
Bring you everlasting comfort
And the joys that never cease.

❋　❋　❋

Keep Christ in Christmas
and He Will Keep You in His Care

If we keep Christ in Christmas
He will keep us every day,
And when we are in His keeping
And we follow in His way
All our little earthly sorrows,
All our worry and our care
Seem lifted from our shoulders
When we go to God in prayer.

This Is the Savior of the World

Some regard the Christmas story
      as something beautiful to hear,
A lovely Christmas custom
      that we celebrate each year.
But it's more than just a story
      told to make our hearts rejoice,
It's our Father up in heaven
      speaking through the Christ Child's voice
Telling us of heavenly kingdoms
      that He has prepared above
For those who put their trust
      in His mercy and His love.
And only through the Christ Child
      can man be born again,
For God sent the Baby Jesus
      as the Savior of all men.

❄   ❄   ❄

A Christmas Meditation

Give us through the coming year
Quietness of mind,
Teach us to be patient
And always to be kind,
Give us reassurance
When everything goes wrong
So our faith remains unfaltering
And our hope and courage strong.
And show us that in quietness
We can feel Your presence near
Filling us with joy and peace
Throughout the coming year.

❄ ❄ ❄

A Pattern for Living

Christmas is more than a day
    at the end of year,
More than a season of joy and good cheer,
    Christmas is really
    God's pattern for living
To be followed all year by unselfish giving.
    For the holiday season
    awakens good cheer
And draws us closer to those we hold dear,
    And we open our hearts
    and find it is good
To live among men as we always should.
    But as soon as the tinsel
    is stripped from the tree
The spirit of Christmas fades silently
    Into the background
    of daily routine

And is lost in the whirl of life's busy scene,
      And all unawares
      we miss and forgo
The greatest blessing that mankind
      can know.
For if we lived Christmas each day,
      as we should,
And made it our aim to always do good,
      We'd find the lost key
      to meaningful living
That comes not from getting, but from unselfish giving.
      And we'd know the great joy
      of peace upon earth
Which was the real purpose of our Savior's birth,
      For in the glad tidings
      of the first Christmas night,
God showed us
      The way and the truth and the light!

❄   ❄   ❄

The Blessed Assurance of Christmas

In the wondrous Christmas story
    a troubled world can find
Blessed reassurance
    and enduring peace of mind —
For though we grow discouraged
    in the world we're living in,
There is comfort just in knowing
    that God triumphed over sin
By sending us His only Son
    to live among us here
So He might know and understand
    man's loneliness and fear —
And for our soul's salvation
    Christ was born and lived and died,
For life became immortal
    when God's Son was crucified,
And the Christ Child's resurrection
    was God's way of telling men
That in Christ we are eternal
    and in Him we live again —
And to know that life is endless
    puts new purpose in our days

And fills our hearts with joyous songs
    of hope and love and praise.
For to know that through the Christ Child
    our spirits were redeemed
And that God has stored up treasures
    beyond all that man has dreamed
Is a promise that is priceless
    and it's ours if we but say
That in so far as in us lies
    we will follow in His way –
For God our Heavenly Father
    and Christ, His only Son,
Will forgive us our transgressions
    and the misdeeds we have done
If we but yield our hearts to God
    and ask but one reward –
The joy of walking daily
    in the footsteps of the Lord.

❄   ❄   ❄

Each Christmas God Renews His Promise

Long, long ago in a land far away,
    There came the dawn
    of the first Christmas Day,
And each year we see that promise reborn
    That God gave the world
    on that first Christmas morn.
For the silent stars in the timeless skies
    And the wonder
    in a small child's eyes,
The Christmas songs the carollers sing,
    The tidings of joy
    that the Christmas bells ring
Remind us again of that still, silent night
    When the heavens shone
    with a wondrous light,
And the angels sang of peace on earth
    And told men of
    the Christ Child's birth –
For Christmas is more than a beautiful story,
    It's the promise of life
    and eternal glory.

Let Us Pray
on This Holy Christmas Day

What better time
And what better season,
What greater occasion
Or more wonderful reason
To kneel down in prayer
And lift our hands high
To the God of Creation
Who made land and sky.
And, oh, what a privilege
As the new year begins
To ask God to wipe out
Our errors and sins
And to know when we ask,
If we are sincere,
He will wipe our slate clean
As we start a new year.
So at this glad season
When joy's everywhere,
Let us meet our Redeemer
At the altar of prayer.

A Christmas Blessing for You

May Jesus, our Savior,
Who was born on Christmas Day,
Bless you at this season
In a very special way.
May the beauty and the promise
Of that silent, holy night
Fill your heart with peace and happiness
And make your new year bright!

O God, Our Help in Ages Past

O God, our help in ages past,
Our hope in years to be,
Look down upon this present
And see our need of Thee.
For in this age of unrest,
With danger all around,
We need Thy hand to lead us
To higher, safer ground.
We need Thy help and counsel
To make us more aware
That our safety and security
Lie solely in Thy care.
And so we pray this Christmas
To feel Thy presence near
And for Thy all-wise guidance
Throughout the coming year.
First, give us understanding
Enough to make us kind,
So we may judge all people
With our heart and not our mind,
Then give us strength and courage
To be honorable and true

And place our trust implicitly
In unseen things and You.
So help us when we falter
And renew our faith each day,
Forgive our human errors
And hear us when we pray,
And keep us gently humble
In the greatness of Thy love
So someday we are fit to dwell
With Thee in peace above.

A Christmas Devotion

O Father, up in heaven
We have wandered far away
From the Holy little Christ Child
Who was born on Christmas Day.
And the peace on earth You promised
We have been unmindful of,
Not believing we could find it
In a simple thing called love.
We've forgotten why You sent us
Jesus Christ, Your only Son,
And in arrogance and ignorance
It's our will, not Thine, be done.
And, O God, in Thy great goodness
May our guidance Christmas night
Be the star the Wise Men followed –
Not a man-made satellite.

❋   ❋   ❋

Behold, I Bring You Good Tidings

What does this mean to us this night,
Just a season that is bright,
A gift ... a greeting of good cheer,
The ending of another year?

How little we have understood
The meaning as we really should.
Our minds and hearts have been so small,
We never got the real meaning at all!

For in these tidings all men received
Much more than they have ever conceived,
For in these words, beyond all seeing,
We live and move and have our being.

A Prayer for Christmas

God give us eyes this Christmas
    to see the Christmas star,
And give us ears to hear the song
    of angels from afar.
And, with our eyes and ears attuned
    for a message from above,
Let Christmas angels speak to us
    of hope and faith and love.
Hope to light our pathway
    when the way ahead is dark,
Hope to sing through stormy days
    with the sweetness of the lark,
Faith to trust in things unseen
    and know beyond all seeing
That it is in our Father's love
    we live and have our being,
And love to break down barriers
    of color, race, and creed,
Love to see and understand
    and help all those in need.

Let Us Seek God's Guidance
in the New Year

As the threatening clouds of chaos
Gather in man's muddled mind
While he searches for an answer
He alone can never find,
May God turn our vision skyward
So that we can see above
The gathering clouds of darkness
And behold God's brightening love —
For today we're facing problems
Man alone can never solve,
For it takes much more than genius
To determine and resolve
The condition that confront us
All around on every side,
Daily mounting in intensity
Like the restless, rising tide —

But we'll find new strength and wisdom
If instead of proud resistance
We humbly call upon the Lord
And seek Divine Assistance,
For the spirit can unravel
Many tangled, knotted threads
That defy the skill and power
Of the world's best hands and heads —
And the plans of growth and progress
Of which we all have dreamed
Cannot survive materially
Unless the spirit is redeemed —
So as another new year dawns
Let us seek the Lord in prayer
And place our future hopes and plans
Securely in God's care.

A Prayer for the New Year

God grant us this year a wider view
So we see others' faults through the eyes of You –
Teach us to judge not with hasty tongue,
Neither the adult . . . nor the young,
Give us patience and grace to endure
And a stronger faith so we feel secure,
And instead of remembering, help us forget
The irritations that caused us to fret
Freely forgiving for some offense
And finding each day a rich recompense
In offering a friendly, helping hand
And trying in all ways to understand
That all of us whoever we are
Are trying to reach an unreachable star –
For the great and small . . . the good and bad,
The young and old . . . the sad and glad
Are asking today, 'Is life worth living?'
And the answer is only in loving and giving –
For only love can make man kind
And kindness of heart brings peace of mind,
And by giving love we can start this year
To lift the clouds of hate and fear.

My Wish

Show me the way,
        not to fortune and fame,
Not how to win laurels
        or praise for my name –
But show me the way
        to spread the great story,
That Thine is the kingdom
        and power and glory.

HSR

❄ ❄ ❄

My Hope

Christmas encompasses all that you've just read
        but the very special part
        is glorifying God
        by the service of your life
        and the thanks within your heart.

VJR